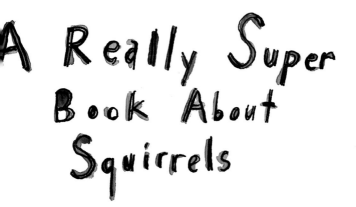

A Really Super
Book About
Squirrels

For information, write
Andrews McMeel Publishing
an Andrews McMeel Universal company
4520 Main Street, Kansas City,
Missouri 64111.

06 07 WKT 10 9 8 7 6 5 4 3

ISBN-13: 978-0-7407-3177-8
ISBN-10: 0-7407-3177-7

ATTENTION:
SCHOOLS AND BUSINESSES

Andrews McMeel books are available
at quantity discounts with bulk purchase
for educational, business, or sales
promotional use.

For information, please write to:
Special Sales Department
Andrews McMeel Publishing
4520 Main Street, Kansas City
Missouri 64111.

A Really Super Book About Squirrels

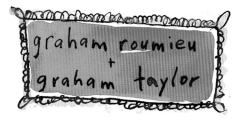

graham roumieu
+
graham taylor

**Andrews McMeel
Publishing**

Kansas City

About the author

Graham Taylor likes squirrels and is happy to have written a book about one. He is currently working on his next literary escapade; a trilogy entitled Cussin', Spittin', + Feudin'. He also likes making movies.

About the illustrator

Graham Roumieu has been drawing pictures for many years and has failed to sell any. Some people will not even take them as gifts. He has no other skills or pastimes to speak of.

About the Squirrel

Little is known about Jimmy the Squirrel as he is a Squirrel and is unable to talk. Through a series of squeaks and chirps he seemed to express that he is excited about having a book written about him and he urges kids to stay in School.

Oh Squirrel
We live so close,
yet we cannot be friends
Sometimes I see you
Sitting on the fence
Eating
           and I think
You would make a good friend.
When I try to give you a nut,
You run away

Why do you bury your food in the ground?
Wouldn't it get dirty?
How do you know where to look when you get
   hungry?
I keep my food in a cupboard.
Even though sometimes I can't find what I want
   I know it is there.
Maybe you too could keep your food in a
   cupboard.
I'd help you get stuff off the top shelf.
Just give it a thought.

← a peanut

Sometimes while walking I see you cross
the street.
You run to the middle and then stop as if
you've forgotten something.
What is it I wonder.
You look back and forth to see if it is safe
to continue, or if you should go back.
Just run I think, a car is coming.
You decide to go and make it
this time.
This whole procedure strikes me as strange.
I was taught to look both ways before
I cross a street.

another
peanut

I'm going to bed now.
Are you sleeping?
Do you have **a bed time**?
Do you dream of bigger and better trees
                         to jump from?
Larger fences to sit on?
More nuts to eat?
I like it when I dream of you Squirrel

or a peanut butter sandwic

Squirrel, can I come over to your house today?
You seem to visit me a lot, I figure it is
time to be as kind.
We could play board games and listen to the
music you like.
Where do you live?
Is it near by?
Is it hard to get to?
Maybe you're just afraid your house isn't clean
enough to have guests over?
I don't think you should worry, I'm not too picky.
And anyways I'll give you an hours notice
starting now.
I'll be waiting on the big branch.

So you're trying to get into the attic.
I hear you chewing through the wood.
I went up there once and don't know why you're tryin
to get in.
It's cold and dark.
There's nothing really up there.
Maybe you were just trying to hide your present
for me.
Don't act suprised, I know you got me a present.
It wasn't necessary, but thank you all the same.
Next time just ring the doorbell and I'll let
you in the front door.

It's sure to save some time.

The ground is beginning to thaw.
The snow is disappearing and you're
        out and about.
I was wondering if I'd see you again.
    There you are.
You must be looking for buried treasure -
        'cause you're digging a lot.
Did you find a treasure map?
What is treasure to you squirrel?
I'm not sure but I'll help you find it.
Wait and I'll get a shovel.
        There's plenty of yard left to dig.

There you are squirrel around the tree
I see you poking your head out
I walk around to say hello but you're gone
Where did you go?
You're on the other side of the tree now.
It's like you're trying to hide from me.
Why would you do that?
Now things are getting out of hand.
Is this some cruel game?
I'm not having fun.
I see you poke your head out at me again
Last chance
Again to the other side
Fun is fun ———— but I've had enough.
  I'm leaving.
Next time don't play your squirrel games.

Hey squirrel where are you?
I'm looking out the window but you're not there
Not sitting on the fence.
Not jumping from branch to branch.
Not filling your cheeks with nuts.
You haven't moved, have you?
I brought a bag of nuts to share
I thought we could sit on the deck,
chew some nuts
and discuss what is weighing us down.
I'll sit ⸺ and wait ⸺ and think of you
And if you don't show
I'll leave you a nut for later.

I'm running.
I'm late.
I don't have time to stand still.
But there you are squirrel.
Sitting on the fence so still.
So calm.
I don't have time for you today squirrel.
I have to go
I turn around and you're gone.
I'm sorry squirrel.
I miss you already.

Brrr, you look cold sitting on that fence with the Sno
Why are you out on a cold day like this?
I like to keep inside with a hot drink.
You stay out in the freezing cold with only your
        tail to keep you warm.
I think you are crazy.
You should have stayed in bed.
Then I realize how much I don't know about
        you squirrel and just how different we are.

Notes about Squirrels

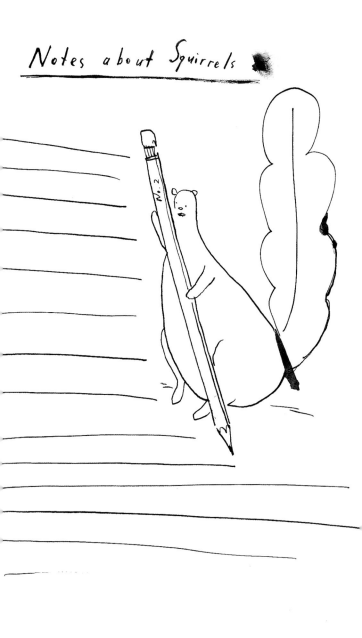